THE LIFE
AND
TIMES OF

ROBESPIERRE

PAUL HAMLYN
London · New York · Sydney · Toronto

FRANCE BEHEADED

On the morning of January 21, 1793 Paris was awake early, although there were few signs of activity in the rainy dawn, later to change into a day of sombre mistiness. The French capital was about to witness the most tragic scene ever enacted in its long and stormy history. The revolutionaries had staged a great display of force; about 30,000 armed men were on the look-out for surprise attacks from within or without. All was in readiness for the action which would set a bloody seal on the farewell to France as a monarchy and to the living symbol of that monarchy, the ex-king Louis XVI. Movement was restricted; doors and windows were closed along the route from the Temple prison to the Place de la République, where the waiting crowds were held back by lines of troops, drawn up in a square around the guillotine. Nevertheless, behind the shutters and within the gates of this seemingly dead city, one could almost feel the vibrations of alarm. This momentous occasion might mask unknown dangers and kindle unsuspected passions. But the execution was swift and nothing happened. Those who had decreed it were far away. They waited for the usual impersonal statement, assembled at their various meeting-places, at the Convention, on committees and in the clubs where they had their permanent seats. The topic of their discussions was not the death of the king, already unimportant, but the killing on the previous day of one of their members whose death had left an empty place. The guillotine had simultaneously beheaded the king and the France of the past. As he prepared himself for death Louis XVI had confirmed to his confessor his belief in the divine right of kings: "Dear God, how thankful I am for my principles. Without them where should I be now? I am certain that up there is an incorruptible Judge who will accord me the justice which men have denied me". Another "incorruptible", a mortal one, had been largely responsible for the fate of the King on earth – a man whom the revolutionaries and the common people alike regarded with unbounded admiration. His name was Maximilien François Isidore de Robespierre and henceforth he was to influence decisively the destiny of France. He was shrewd and politically adroit; and above all he was "incorruptible".

Left page: Louis XVI's farewell to his family. This page, far left: last portrait of Louis XVI, drawn three days before his execution. The artist, Ducreux, was one of the commissioners charged with the security of the prisoner. The King was 39 but appears prematurely aged. Left: a print of "Louis the Last" and his family in the Temple prison. The republican red cap of liberty is being replaced by the green one of the convict. Below: the executioner, Sanson, displays the King's severed head from the scaffold. Louis XVI made a dignified speech to the crowd but it was drowned by the roll of drums ordered by Santerre of the Convention.

Left: Robespierre's house at Arras, his home town, with which he was associated throughout his life. Right: Robespierre as a young man; his sister, Charlotte, to whom we owe many anecdotes of the life of the "Incorruptible"; a portrait of Rousseau by Allan Ramsay. Below: the awakening of the Third Estate, from a contemporary print.

REVEIL DU TIERS ETAT.

TOP OF THE CLASS

Below: a detail from Couder's painting of the meeting of the States-General at Versailles, with Robespierre in the foreground. He was slender and elegant but his delicate appearance belied his inner strength. Late nights and hard work accentuated his pallor while his nervous debility manifested itself in facial contortions. Even at the height of the Terror Robespierre retained his bourgeois habits; he wore knee breeches, a long coat and shirts with embroidered wristbands and lace fronts. To the end of his life his hair was powdered in the style of the ancien régime and he never appeared in the red cap of liberty.

Like many celebrated revolutionaries, Robespierre came from a good middle-class family, one of the so-called *noblesse de la robe*. For many years he prefixed his name with the aristocratic *"de"*. His father was a lawyer in Arras, in the Artois, whose marriage to Jacqueline Marguerite Carraut was something of an afterthought; their eldest child, Maximilien, was born on May 6, 1758, only four months after the wedding. He had one brother, Augustin, five years younger, who would be at his side during the searing days of revolution; there was a sister, Charlotte, who survived him long enough to recount the fortunes of the family, and another sister, Henriette. His mother died in childbirth when Maximilien was seven years old and his father deserted the children and died abroad. The two boys were put in the care of their maternal grandfather, who sent them to a nearby convent school. Having completed his early education locally Maximilien attracted the notice of the bishop, who got him a scholarship to the *Collège de Louis-le-Grand,* the best grammar school in Paris. Some of his fellow students here were later to play a leading part along with him in the Revolution, the best known being Fréron and Camille Desmoulins. The fact that he was an orphan, whose schooling was provided by charity, probably increased his natural reserve. He was, however, an excellent student and fully deserved his place at the top of the class. On the occasion of Louis XVI's visit to the school it was Maximilien who was chosen to deliver an official address in Latin verse. Because of his classical education he was familiar with stories of heroes and of enemies of tyranny; he was also inspired by the ideals of Jean-Jacques Rousseau. In 1781 he left his Paris college and returned to Arras to practise law. His dress and manners were already impeccable; he wrote lightheartedly to pretty ladies about their lapdogs and canaries. Then everything was changed by the convocation of the States-General. Using his own family as a political committee, Robespierre got himself elected as one of the deputies of the Third Estate and attended the meeting at Versailles on May 5, 1789. Like a number of other delegates he had already written an excellent pamphlet demanding reform.

THE TORCH OF PROVENCE AND THE CANDLE OF ARRAS

Although the States-General soon took the title of National Assembly, the accord between the monarchy and its delegates seemed likely to continue. Robespierre himself saw in Louis XVI the man destined to bring about a revolution "which, in advance of their times, Henry IV and Charles the Great had attempted without success". But his somewhat clumsy eloquence did not inspire his fellow representatives. There even seems to have been a deliberate attempt to distort his name. He is variously reported as "Robertspierre", "Robert-Pierre" and sometimes "Robez Pierre". The Assembly was dominated by Gabriel Honoré de Riqueti, Comte de Mirabeau, fugitive from the aristocracy and self-ordained standard-bearer of the Third Estate. In a contemporary journal, the *Actes des Apôtres,* a writer commented: "If Monsieur Mirabeau is the torch of Provence then Monsieur de Robespierre is just a candle from Arras". The comparison was malicious but apt. Mirabeau burned with a bright but restless fire, whose blaze was often dimmed by the smoke of his imperfections; Robespierre's small flame was colder and clearer, more constant and precise. The candle would still be alight when the torch had ceased to burn.

Left: portrait of Mirabeau by Boze. Born in 1749, Mirabeau belonged to the aristocracy of Provence. He became the leading figure in the National Assembly and his death, on April 2, 1791, was regarded as a national disaster. Above, left: Mirabeau's reply to the King's Messenger. The event portrayed occurred at the dissolution of the States-General on June 23, 1789. Louis XVI announced that the delegates must vote separately according the the three estates – nobility, clergy and Third Estate – and not by a majority of the three. When commanded to leave the hall Mirabeau defied the order in the name of the Third Estate. Above right: David's famous painting of the Tennis Court Oath (June 20, 1789). On the opposite page: a detail from the same work showing Robespierre clutching his breast.

Days of feverish excitement preceded the storming of the Bastille. The mob overran the square on the night of July 12 – 13 (as Prieur's print on the left shows). Two decisive events followed: the setting up of a revolutionary body to replace the old administration and the formation of a national guard, which rapidly mustered 12,000 men. A standing committee headed this movement and the streets of Paris were patrolled throughout the night of July 13–14. On the morning of July 14 the demonstrators, encouraged by the passivity of the troops, went to Les Invalides, where they looted the palace and armed themselves with rifles and cannons. The painting by Lallemand (above) shows the culmination of this raid, which made possible the attack on the Bastille. The Paris mob, drawing together men from every walk of life, and inspiring great fear, itself stood in dread of reactionary plots. The tumult continued throughout the night of July 14 – 15 (Prieur's engraving, far right). Meanwhile there was dancing round the tree of liberty (right).

THE PEOPLE OF PARIS BECOME A RABBLE

The members of the Third Estate who assembled at Versailles were chiefly Frenchmen from country districts who felt that their rights had been neglected and abused by their rulers in Paris. The peasants especially believed that there was a plot against them: that a privileged few were conspiring to deprive them of their rights. This old belief in an aristocratic plot, ever active in the countryside, now grew and swelled the discontents of the city artisans who were the main victims of the recurrent economic crisis. Like the other delegates, Robespierre was resolved that the provinces should finally have a voice in national affairs. Even before he left Arras he had told a local cobbler that great changes were coming. But like some others he preferred to modify the old order rather than to overthrow it. Then things changed. At Versailles the delegates talked; in Paris the mob acted, and the disorders culminated in the storming of the Bastille. July 14, 1789, was the first of the great "days" of the revolution, swift dramas which, in a few hours of Paris rioting, changed the face of France. As the movement gathered momentum and spread from the provinces to the capital it suddenly took on a new aspect. Paris was crowded with political cafes and groups. Arguments raged in the *Salon des Arts,* in the Military Assembly and in the Valois Circle. At Versailles the deputies chose to lodge at the same inn as others from their province (for this reason Robespierre stayed at the Volpe Hotel) and by night they prepared and continued the debates begun in the council chamber. But the trauma resulting from the "day" of July 14, gave rise to unforeseen consequences. The capture of the Bastille was not momentous in itself; its importance as a fortress was chiefly symbolic, and the surprise of the defenders probably exceeded the valour of the attackers. Its significance lay in the mob's realization of its own strength and of how it could be exploited. It was the signal for the beginning of a period when the people's obsession, or intoxication, perhaps, with this new-found power led them to ever-increasing violence and cruelty. Robespierre summed up the situation: "We have our liberty and a little blood has been shed. To be sure some heads have fallen – but they were guilty heads. . . . So, gentlemen, it is to this rebellion that the nation owes its liberty".

THE "HIGH PRIEST" OF THE NATION

Prints on this and opposite page: two incidents from the provincial uprisings: the massacre of the patriots at Montauban (May 10, 1790) and the mutiny of the ships Léopard *and* Amérique *at Brest (September, 1790). Robespierre championed the patriots, soldiers and sailors in revolt, and pleaded for clemency.*

Below: two coloured prints reflecting the harmony brought about by the National Assembly. Left: actresses giving jewels and money to the patriotic fund; right: the three estates co-operating to forge the constitution. Opposite, right: the market women marching on Versailles (October 5, 1789). Note the men in disguise.

In the Guild Hall of Paris the new authorities were installed under the Mayor, Bailly. Suddenly a new force appeared and rapidly took over the leading rôle. This was the Paris Commune and it soon overshadowed the Assembly. The monarchy was carried along in its wake, however, and the popular demonstrations, not yet conspicuously anti-monarchist, lost their impetus. On July 17 the King agreed to replace his white cockade with the tricoloured one, symbol of the nation's rebirth; on August 26 he ratified the Declaration of the Rights of Man and of the Citizen, which the Assembly had passed on the previous day. Earlier, on the night of August 4, the nobility and clergy, the rivals of the Third Estate, had been deprived of their privileges. (This was more declared intent than accomplishment, as it was not until four years later, in July 1793, that their privileges were finally and totally abolished.) Meanwhile the Paris crowds founded and organized the National Guard; it was led by La Fayette, veteran of the American wars and known as the "hero of two worlds". The women of the Paris markets marched to Versailles and there demanded that the royal family should return with them to Paris. This was the second great revolutionary "day", October 5, and it ended in rejoicing and singing as the King, the Queen and the Dauphin were installed in the Tuileries, along with the Assembly, on whose meetings the attention of the capital was focussed. Voices raised there found a wider and more responsive audience, quick to identify itself with the issues discussed. Among them that of Robespierre began to be heard. He was delicate in physique and unassuming in his olive-coloured clothes; his voice, normally hoarse and feeble, would rise to a near falsetto when he was excited; he was highly strung and his face was frequently contorted. But he took upon himself the rôle of champion of the oppressed and neglected; while defending the negroes of San Domingo against Barnave he declared uncompromisingly that it was "better to lose the colonies than to sacrifice a single principle". He specialized in anti-Catholic lawsuits, especially those brought by protestants and Jews, for whom he demanded equality of rights, and he was always ready to defend actors. He was, in short, the high priest, "the Levite of the nation".

THE MAN WHO BELIEVED ALL HE SAID

In the Assembly, which had now moved from the Tuileries to the royal riding school, the talking went on. Between May and December of the year 1789 twenty-five attendances by Robespierre are recorded. In addition he made 42 replies to speeches by Barnave, 75 to Target and 122 to Mirabeau. From Mirabeau, at least, the little lawyer from Arras attracted special notice. "He will go far" he commented, "because he believes in everything he himself says." This sarcasm was an unintentional compliment. As a politician, Mirabeau certainly outshone Robespierre, who seemed ingenuous by comparison. But Robespierre, to his lasting credit, was a man of integrity and never preached what he did not practise. This explains his ascendancy, for in other respects he was not generously endowed by nature and he was more a man of the lobbies than of the Assembly, more of the clubs than of the genuine tribune. He conquered by his steadfast championship of democratic principles. Since September 1789 and the debate against the monarch's right to veto, which some wanted suspended and others made absolute, he had moved to the left of Barnave and Mirabeau and ranged himself alongside the extremists,

exemplified by Marat. He chiefly attracted attention, however, by his strict logic and ruthlessly legal mind. In his own words: "Whoever asserts that one man has the right to oppose the law says that the will of one man is superior to the will of all. He declares that the nation is of no account and that one man is all-important. If he adds that this right belongs to him who is invested with executive power, he is saying that the man elevated by the people to carry out the will of the people has the right to oppose and enslave the will of the people; he has created an inconceivable monster both morally and politically – and this monster is none other than the royal veto . . ." For the time being he did not prevail, but the portents were there. He became the laughing-stock of the moderates, so much so that at the end of 1789 he was receiving letters from Arras telling him that respectable citizens were ashamed of him. On leaving Versailles he had rented an apartment in the rue de Saintonge, in Paris, where he led a life of seclusion. Here he studied, and prepared his speeches. From 1790 he shared his lodgings with a secretary, Villiers, who worked for him occasionally without payment.

On October 6, 1789 the royal
family moved to the Tuileries and
were welcomed by Paris amid
scenes of rejoicing. (On the
opposite page a contemporary print
of the occasion.) The life of the
capital continued normally, or
almost so, for the majority of its
inhabitants were usually uninterested
spectators of these historic events.
Above, a painting by Senave, in
1791, shows the bank of the Seine in
the neighbourhood of Notre-Dame
bridge, with passers–by, strolling
pedlars and a group of spectators
watching an acrobat. The only
indication of the new régime is the
detachment of guards on the left.
Now and again, however, riots
broke out unexpectedly. The print
on the left shows such an incident:
the sacking of the De Castriés
palace on November 13, 1790.

15

July 14, 1790 was the first
anniversary of the Bastille. The
Assembly and the whole of France
celebrated the Feast of the
Federation in complete harmony.
Below: this mass rally was directed
by La Fayette, heading the National
Guard. Everyone joined in levelling
the ground at the Champ de Mars.
Even Louis XVI wielded a pick

(left). A year later there was a
very different scene (below). An
attempt was made to lay an anti-
Royalist petition on the altar of the
nation. The rally was forbidden and
martial law proclaimed. La
Fayette gave the order to fire and at
least 50 demonstrators were
killed. Right: portrait, by Vaquelin,
of Robespierre in 1791.

16

THE LADIES, THE PRESS AND THE JACOBINS SUPPORT HIM

At the Amaury coffee house in Versailles, a meeting place for political discussion, a seat was reserved for Robespierre. A group called the Breton Club had been formed, for at that time the deputies tended to assemble according to their regions of origin. This was the beginning of the Jacobin Club. Originally the Society of Friends of the Constitution, it had followed the Assembly to Paris and established itself at the library of the Dominicans, popularly nicknamed the Jacobins. Here the middle class revolutionaries met together. Rival groups also flourished; the Cordeliers' Club, for example, the Society for the Rights of Man and Citizen, was led by artisans and discontented tradesmen and shopkeepers. New names became known there: Danton, Marat, Hébert. A dissident group of Jacobins formed, calling themselves the Feuillants. All these groups were animated by hatred of the political parties, which they referred to as "factions". And yet these groups, influencing and controlling their adherents, were really themselves parties in embryo. The Jacobins established a series of branches, provincial clubs with which they were in active correspondence. In time their own name would become synonymous with party extremism. Meanwhile the supporters of the club pledged their loyalty to the Constitution in a solemn statement which began: "I swear to live in freedom or to die". In these surroundings Robespierre found his first real platform and shed the final traces of his provincialism. In March 1790 he was named president of the club and received warm support from his friend Camille Desmoulins. Their friendship dated from their schooldays but now, in addition, there was the backing of Camille's own journal, *Les Révolutions de France et de Brabant.* Those who were aware of Camille's affection for Lucille Duplessis said that he induced Robespierre to ask for the hand of her sister, Adèle. But even in matters of sentiment Robespierre was the image of reserve. Adèle Duplessis was a widow who offered him youth and a fortune, but she stood no chance with him. It is strange that among so many men more dashing and flamboyant than he, Robespierre had great success with the ladies. The former provincial now had three arrows to his bow, the Jacobins, the press and the ladies, three weapons to help him in his political ascent.

THE KING'S FLIGHT MAKES ROBESPIERRE A REPUBLICAN

A new incident now caused a great stir. On the morning of June 21, 1791 the bells of Paris sounded the alarm for a sensational announcement; the King and the royal family had fled. Already political refugees were numerous but, so far, emigration had been simply a convenient way of getting rid of public and private enemies. With the passing of the laws on the civil constitution of the clergy, politics had become a matter of conscience. The flight of the King, intercepted at Varennes, was bedevilled by frustrations and miscalculations. All the same, while the fugitives were being brought back to Paris amidst jeering abuse, an attempt was made to keep up appearances. La Fayette signed the order to return the King under escort and the National Assembly issued an "explanation": the King had been abducted; he had not deserted his subjects. He must be acquitted because of insufficient evidence of guilt. Thus they avoided deposing him and Louis XVI remained as King, but was "suspended". Not unnaturally, many people though the flight to Varennes justified the creation of a republican party. On July 14, 1791, Robespierre made an address which was published but never spoken. In it he said that "the King had dishonoured himself by his perjury" and it was no longer possible for such a king to be reinstated because "the lowest of his subjects would feel dishonoured by him". Then came the real crime. On July 17 a petition demanding the deposition of Louis XVI and the foundation of a republic was laid on the national altar at the Champ de Mars; it was instigated by the popular society backed by the Cordelier club and led by Danton. The Assembly commanded the mayor, Bailly, and the commander of the National Guard, La Fayette, to restore order. *Agents provocateurs* created disorder and the troops fired on the crowd. Robespierre, far from being one of the leaders of the petition, had counselled restraint. But his words of three days previously could now be construed as support for the proposal to dismiss the King and, therefore, for the disorders. It seemed prudent for him to keep out of the way. He avoided the rue de Saintonge for several days. For the time being he accepted the hospitality of the cabinet maker, Maurice Duplay, at 336 rue Saint-Honoré.

Left: an anti-clerical print, "The removal of the clergy". Since 1790, Pope Pius VI had condemned the laws on the civil constitution of the clergy. Louis XVI's conscience was troubled; he dreaded the approach of Easter when he would have to receive communion. Why not leave Paris and join the loyal troops at Metz? His flight was badly organized; his party was recognized at Sainte-Menehoulde and arrested at Varennes about midnight on June 21. On the 25th they were back in Paris (below). A foreign diplomat recorded that, when referring to the King, "the French employ only such words as beast and coward".

The war, unanimously approved by the Legislative Assembly, was at first extremely popular. This is confirmed by the print (below) which shows "The departure of the Citizen" and the painting (opposite page) which depicts a detachment of the National Guard marching off to the front. Wherever the tricolour waved battalions of volunteers formed, bursting with patriotic fervour, but untrained and poorly armed. The old troops of the line of the standing army had already lost 6,000 out of their 9,000 officers through emigration and 30,000 men, chiefly through desertion. The idea of invading Flanders before the Austrian army could be mobilized was daring but doomed to failure. Very soon, on July 11, it had to be admitted that the country was in peril. Below, left and right: Verdun surrenders to the Prussians, and the capture of Spira by the French. In the centre: the events at Avignon (October 1791). The annexation of this papal possession sharpened the conflict with the Holy See.

AT THE OUTBREAK OF WAR HE WAS ALREADY THE "INCORRUPTIBLE"

One of the foundations on which Robespierre had built his growing reputation had been a suggestion of his which made a great impression on public opinion. In his speech of May 16, 1791 he had proposed that no member of the Constituent Assembly should be eligible for re-election to the Legislative Assembly foreseen in the constitution. The proposal was enthusiastically received and carried by an overwhelming majority. Marat, spokesman of the most violent popular group, wrote in his *Ami du peuple*: "We may lose a few honourable deputies, Grégoire, Pétion and especially the incorruptible Robespierre, but we shall no longer need to fear those representatives of the privileged class, more than a few of whom still survive as ruthless enemies of liberty". So now Robespierre had become the "Incorruptible". The constitution was passed and the King took the oath on September 14, 1791, whereupon the Assembly was dissolved. A journey to his native Arras confirmed the popularity of the "Incorruptible", even in the provinces. However, his interests now centred on Paris, and in the Jacobin club which had become the driving force of the revolution, a revolution which Robespierre did not regard as fully accomplished. In control of the new assembly were the men who would later be known as Girondins, but were then called "Brissotins" after their leader, Brissot. The depreciating value of the *assignats,* the paper money guaranteed by national property, and the resultant inflation, were signs of increasing internal difficulties. Moreover, the French revolution had already become an international affair and foreign rulers were threatening to attack the frontier. A patriotic appeal to repel outside enemies could be an effective distraction from internal problems. It was therefore decided, on April 20, 1792, to declare war on the Emperor of Germany, whose forces were supported by those of the King of Prussia. Robespierre was strongly opposed to this; he was not interested in war, for to him the Revolution was all-important and not to be relegated to second place by conflict with other nations. "War is what we should most fear", he had declared from the Jacobin platform. After the first flushes of patriotism, events seemed to prove him right and his prestige and political powers increased accordingly.

Two pictures below: meeting of a popular women's club in a desecrated church, and the interior of a Paris club. The Jacobins extended their influence throughout France, with 152 affiliated societies in 1790 and 400 a year later. The Cordeliers, however, headed by Marat and Danton, played the leading part in the insurrectionary Paris "days". Right-hand page, top: an anti-religious print. The main stages of the conflict against the Church were: July 12 and November 27, 1790 – civil constitution of the clergy and compulsory oath; May to June, 1792 – further restrictive laws against the so called "non-juror" priests. Below: the patriots' coffee house, by Swebach-Desfontaines.

Right: "The triumph of Robespierre and Pétion", from a contemporary print. On September 14, 1791 Louis XVI spoke to the Assembly accepting the constitution. Paris was jubilant and rejoicing broke out at the Guild Hall. Robespierre and Pétion were crowned with oak leaves. Jérôme Pétion de Villeneuve who replaced Bailly as mayor in November, was a member of the Convention and the Committee of Public Safety. A Girondin, he fled in June '93 was hunted down and possibly committed suicide in 1794, at the age of 38.

THE JACOBINS AS THE DRIVING FORCE OF THE REVOLUTION

Although it was elected for two years the Legislative Assembly barely lasted for one, from October 1, 1791 to September 20, 1792. The real leaders of the revolutionary movement, Robespierre, Danton and Marat, had remained outside it because of the order making them ineligible for re-election. It was therefore inevitable that policies should be formed to an increasing extent outside the elected assembly and in the clubs, which were recognized as centres of authority by the deputies of the Legislative Assembly. Of the moderates, 264 sided with the Feuillants, the splinter group of the Jacobins, while 136 supported the left wing of the Jacobins. There remained the others, the majority, who brought the total up to 745 elected representatives. These professed independence but formed, in effect, a huge floating vote between the two opposing factions of the Feuillants and the Jacobins. The liveliness of the latter's ideas and the importance of their leaders made them distinctly superior. All the issues which were brought before the Assembly were discussed among the Jacobins, who prepared, criticized, controlled and often dictated the decisions finally taken. Robespierre had become their president in 1790 and in June 1791 he was commissioned to organize their electoral programme. The real power was at the heart of the club and was vested in the so-called Committee of Correspondence. Behind the facade of meetings, which were held four times a week, the Committee maintained its links with the associated provincial clubs. It called for suggestions, considered them carefully and, if deemed necessary, ratified the various proposals. At the centre of this committee, the backbone of Jacobin policy, was Robespierre himself. He was thus to be found, at one and the same time, in the centre of the stage as well as waiting in the wings. It was apparent to the politically aware that he was becoming more and more the driving force of revolutionary France.

Opposite page, top: "Homage to Liberty", a popular print bearing the verses of a Marseillaise, Below: painting by Boilly of the distribution of provisions, whose shortage was one of the causes of the recurrent disorders. Black market and famine raged, especially during the disastrous winter of 1793–4. Below left: the mob

invades the Tuileries on June 20 and (right) a demonstration celebrating the third anniversary of the storming of the Bastille (July 14, 1792).
Bottom of the page: Louis XVI is forced to don the red cap of liberty. Mayor Pétion's belated intervention released him from this humiliation.

A "DAY" WHICH SERVED AS A DRESS REHEARSAL

Robespierre was one of the few who had been against the war. He had declared: "We shall be betrayed and so defeated or, if we win, the victorious general will become the people's enemy". He was right, as the adventures of Bonaparte were later to prove; but the deputies, and especially those who were followers of Brissot, were bent on war. When the first setbacks happened it seemed expedient to concentrate on the enemy within. Following the promptings of the Jacobin club they proposed new measures, aimed at curtailing what little authority the monarchy still possessed. The sovereign's escort was to be dismissed, "refractory" priests (those who would not take the oath to the new régime) were to be banished, and a force of 20,000 national guards was to be brought in from the provinces. Louis XVI accepted the first provision but vetoed the other two. This resulted in the fall of the Girondin ministry. To force the King's hand a revolutionary "day" was planned. Robespierre distrusted this plan and disapproved of the demonstration of force which the Brissotins, together with sections of the Paris Commune, had fixed for June 20, 1792. Pretending that they were going to plant a tree of liberty on the anniversary of the Tennis Court Oath, the demonstrators, 8–10,000 strong, armed themselves with picks and went to the Tuileries. Then they despatched a delegation to the hall where the Assembly was meeting and broke into the royal apartments. The The King was forced to put on a red cap of liberty and drink the health of the nation until Pétion, the mayor of Paris, intervened to release him. The "day" was unsuccessful but it had been a useful dress rehearsal.

Below: "The fearful night of August 10 in Paris". Above, left to right, other incidents of the rebellion: Louis XIV's statue being pulled down during the August riots; the attack on the Tuileries (detail from the painting by Bertaux) and the siege of the Tuileries (contemporary print). Troops from Marseilles, brought to Paris on July 14, formed the backbone of the attack. Previously the Commune had dismissed Mandat, the commander of the Tuileries National Guard, and he was murdered by the mob. The Swiss Guard capitulated after two hours and the insurgents killed 600 out of a total of 900. They themselves lost 376.

AUGUST 10, 1792 — ROBESPIERRE SEIZES HIS CHANCE

Although lacking many political qualities Robespierre possessed one which clearly raised him far above his colleagues – his sense of timing. He had been hostile to the exceptional measures favoured by the Brissotins because he feared that public order could be used as a pretext to stifle the Revolution. "Why," he demanded, "should I need to prove to you that the safety of the country and the well-being of the nation require exceptional measures . . . when it is simply a case of our representatives doing strictly what is necessary in the present situation? All I am asking is that you should punish a Court which has intrigued and generals who have betrayed you." But his scruples were to fade away under pressure of events, and choosing his time perfectly, he abandoned the rearguard where he had prudently stationed himself for the abortive "day" of June 20, and took up his position in the van. For a short time he had been pushed aside by the Girondins; soon it would be his turn to rout them. The fear of a military dictatorship reconciled him provisionally to the Brissotins. The Festival of the Federation on July 14, 1792, and the setting up of the insurrectionary Paris Commune, were stages of this reconciliation. The bands of Federals being sent in from the provinces and the disturbances in the Paris sections foreshadowed the "day" of August 10, 1792. There were many, including Danton, Camille Desmoulins, Marat and Fabre d'Eglantine, who were convinced that the only way to defeat the sovereigns of Europe now waging war on France was first to rid themselves of the king they had at home. Robespierre elaborated on this. He maintained that the evil emanated from the Assembly as well as from the King and his advisers. In the coming struggle to set the Commune, a new political power based on popular support, against the elected National Assembly, Robespierre sided with the Commune. Danton and his men carried out the planned attack on August 10; but, though theirs was the physical force, the brain behind them was Robespierre's. When the Tuileries was stormed by the mob and the Assembly voted to suspend the King, the Commune insisted that it should have custody of him. By now Robespierre had abandoned the last of his scruples and was siding openly with the most violent of the revolutionaries.

Below: after the fall of the monarchy which he had tried so consistently to save, La Fayette left his headquarters at Sedan and fled the country, on August 19, 1792. Foot of page: anonymous portrait of Danton. He was brutal and violent, unrestrained in his speech, capable of bold deeds and dubious compromises. The wife of his colleague, Roland, called him "the Mirabeau of the riff-raff". Madame Roland was a woman of a philosophical spirit and refined manners and she found him insufferable. Opposite page: an incident from the savage massacres at the Abbaye prison, which began on September 2, 1792 and continued for four days.

DANTON'S VIOLENCE IN FULL SWING

Once Louis XVI was really deposed it became necessary to govern somehow. Two thirds of the deputies of the Legislative Assembly deserted their seats in terror. The Commune was triumphant and legality was suspended. Danton, the leading figure of these days, was content to leave the Assembly in existence since it no longer had any importance. He was brought on to the six-man executive council as Minister of Justice and easily imposed his own will on the ex-Girondin ministers in the government. The results were threefold: a convention was elected by universal suffrage; relatives of émigrés and other suspects were hunted down: and a revolutionary tribunal was inaugurated. In many respects Danton was the antithesis of Robespierre, although both were lawyers and provincials who had uprooted themselves to come to Paris (Danton was from Arcis-sur-Aube). "When a ship founders the crew jettisons the ballast", he proclaimed. The "ballast" in this case was the prisoners who filled the Paris jails by order of the Commune, and between September 2 and 6 eleven hundred of them were savagely massacred in the name of the People by a handful of assassins. The responsibility was everybody's and yet nobody's but the blame fell chiefly on the leader at that time, Danton. Robespierre did not betray himself but simply commented that it was "necessary to *colérer* and enlighten the *sansculottes*". "*Colérer*", a word invented by him, is far more expressive than simply "enrage". The results of this artificially created enragement were not long in showing themselves.

On 20 September, 1792, Valmy (right) was given over to an artillery battle. The French lost only 300 men, the Prussians even fewer, but it brought tremendous political prestige for it was the first republican victory (the Convention assembled on the 21 September). Below: this satirical print mocks the Prussian retreat.

30

NO LONGER THE CANDLE OF ARRAS BUT THE CHIEF TRIBUNE OF PARIS

The vogue for things republican quickly spread from dress into other fields. Kings and queens disappeared from packs of cards and were replaced by symbolic figures such as Equality and Fraternity (below: contemporary playing cards). Cities, streets and people were renamed. The republican calendar abolished the saints, and children born under the new rule were called Rhubarb, Chicory or Donkey. It was compulsory to employ the familiar "tu" in place of the formal "vous". The only person who did not adopt such exaggerated forms was Robespierre. A sketch from life shows him on the rostrum, impeccable as always.

The election of the Convention, from September 2–20, passed almost unnoticed in the provinces but caused tumult in Paris, already excited by the September massacres. There were 7 million electors out of 25 million inhabitants and about 6,300,000 abstained. When the Convention assembled there were only 371 members present in the chamber out of 749. The Convention abolished the monarchy on September 21 and proclaimed the next day the first of "Year I of the Republic". On the 25th it declared the Republic to be "one and indivisible". There had been a steady movement to the left. The extremists of yesterday, the Girondins led by Brissot, were now the moderates. There were 165 of them against a hundred Jacobins and Cordeliers, known as the *Montagnards* – the "Mountain" – because they occupied the upper seats in the Assembly. The Brissotins had the support of the provinces but they had lost Paris. The revolution had previously ebbed and flowed between the capital and the country but now it belonged to Paris and was anchored to the Commune. By attacking first Marat, then Danton and finally Robespierre, the Girondins had only united the three on a temporary but effective common front. The "Incorruptible" waited for his chance. On November 5 he took the floor and succeeded in identifying his cause with that of the populace. "Do you," he demanded, "want a revolution without revolution?" He vindicated himself simply by requesting "the return of peace and the triumph of liberty". No longer was Robespierre just a "candle of Arras". Deprived of the external attributes of a tribune, he was now the supertribune and a force to reckon with.

THE IMPERTURBABLE ROBESPIERRE'S WEAPONS – SPEECHES AND PAMPHLETS

The opening of the republican Convention coincided with the French army defeating (though only temporarily) the Prussians and Austrians. General Dumouriez's two victories, first at Valmy on September 20, then at Jemappes on November 6, greatly encouraged the revolutionaries, dismayed the monarchists and persuaded the hesitant to support the conquerors. Robespierre and his adherents now increased their insistence that the time had come to decide the fate of the King. Robespierre was by this time the undisputed leader of the Jacobins, who, since the "day" of August 10, had adopted the title of "Friends of Liberty and Equality". Robespierre saw the opportunity which now presented itself. He made good use of the weapons he had at his disposal, his speeches and writings, to forward his plans. Since May 1792 he had been publishing a journal of his own. *Lé défenseur de la Constitution* (The defender of the Constitution), which later became the *Lettres à ses commettants* (Letters to his constituents). This publication greatly increased the influence of his voice. Besides this, his popularity had spread far beyond the confines of Paris. A young man who was to be devoted to him, Saint-Just, wrote to him at the end of August, 1790: "You whom I know, like God, only by your marvellous works . . . ." Other letters poured in from Avignon, Marseilles and Toulon, providing valuable material for his discussions. In common with most other journals of the time his paper was actually a series of pamphlets appearing at more or less regular intervals. The articles resembled rebellious speeches addressed to the reader, contrasting with his actual speeches, which were always drawn up in minute detail like written articles. In this he was only following the current practice. When he mounted the rostrum he assumed a cold, impassive calmness. His gestures were carefully deliberate; he would raise his hand to his heart as though to confirm the sincerity of his words. He once said: "You do not understand the power of truth and the strength of innocence when they are protected by imperturbable courage". His own imperturbability and the power of his speeches and writings were the weapons employed by this man who most typified the Revolution: the "incorruptible" Robespierre.

Left: on November 6, 1792 there was a new republican victory at Jemappes, this time over the Austrians; it opened the road to Belgium for General Dumouriez, who was 53 years old at the time. He had served under the King and fought in the Seven Years War. He was both an officer and a diplomat and came into conflict with the Convention when he had its envoys arrested (bottom picture). Below: an incident from the guerilla warfare in the Vendée, where there was continuous and bloody fighting along the Loire. Peace was only achieved in 1796 under Hoche, who proved an excellent general and skilful politician. A new monarchist revolt flared up briefly in 1799.

HE IS FORCED TO RIDE THE TIGER OF REVOLUTION

The King was in prison and the Commune was guarding him. The Republic had been proclaimed. What was to be done now with Louis Capet, as they called him? His fate was a gauge by which the luke-warm could be distinguished from the extremists, the true revolutionaries from the false. It also became a weapon in the struggle which the Montagnards, the Jacobins, waged against the Girondins. Madame Roland, their familiar spirit, had been distressed by the September massacres. "You know my love for the Revolution," she wrote, "but this has made me ashamed." The King's head was now a pawn in a game where there was far more at stake than the person of Louis XVI. The Montagnards did not want a trial at all. In his speech of December 3, 1792, Robespierre put the question in plainly political terms and tipped the scales as surely as if he had weighted them with iron: "You are not obliged to have a trial. Louis is not the accused and you are not judges. You are not, and could not be, anything other than men of state and representatives of the people. There is no need of a verdict for or against an individual; all that is expected of you is to provide for public safety, to perform a providential act to safeguard the nation". His arguments were incontrovertible according to revolutionary logic. But the Girondins were equally insistent that the Convention should hold a trial and on this point they got their way. It was only a semblance of an official trial, not a true prosecution of justice, and the result was a foregone conclusion. It began on December 11, 1792 and dragged on until January. On the sixteenth day the final casting of votes began, by name, at Marat's request. A Girondin proposal of a plebiscite on the sentence was rejected and 387 out of a total of 721 voters declared for the death penalty, although 26 of them had reservations. On the next day Brissot again tried for a new adjournment but there was no escape. "It is with sorrow that I pronounce this fatal truth," said Robespierre. "It is better that Louis should die than a hundred thousand upright citizens. Louis must die because the country must live." He had sought to take the irreversible step and he had succeeded. The regicides, with Robspierre at their head, were now astride the revolutionary tiger, and would have to ride it until the end.

Above: the murder of Lepeletier on January 20, 1793. Michel Lepeleiter de Saint-Fargeau, chief magistrate at the beginning of the Revolution, was one of the nobility's deputies in the States-General. Later he was elected to the Convention by the Yonne department. The day after he had voted for the death of the King he was assassinated by one of the royal bodyguard, Pâris, on the eve of the King's execution. Left: Louis XVI and his son in the Temple prison.

34

Far left: the meeting of Marat and Dumouriez (October 16, 1792). Born in 1743, at Boudry, Neuchatel, Jean Paul Marat was a doctor, and thought himself misunderstood as a scientist and inventor. He became a leading figure after the "day" of August 10. His fanaticism made him extremely popular; but he asserted the need for a leader: "fools always go in herds". Left: Marat on April 24, 1793, after his arrest by the Girondins and his acquittal by the revolutionary tribunal.

THE INSATIABLE THIRST OF THE REVOLUTIONARY GODS

The execution of Louis XVI had been a challenge to the Europe of princes. Its aim was twofold, internal and external: to prevent any possibility of a return to the old rule and to proclaim to the rest of the world the arrival of the new order. But where was the new order? And, to start with, would the regicides give back to France a degree of serenity, still less of happiness? The Revolution, constructed for universal power, vowed it would topple all despots from their thrones. The King had been removed because he was declared to be a traitor to the French nation. Louis XVI's call to the other monarchies had been designed to intimidate. It had been a request for help based on ideas of mutual solidarity; it was also something of a family pact because of the ties which bound French monarchy to the other reigning dynasties. But apart from this, the threat of the "Convention's hordes", as the forces of the Republic were called, and their declared intent to annexe new territories and carry their policies beyond their natural confines, which were those of the old monarchy, alarmed the European powers. England only took an interest in the fate of the King on the day the French invaded Belgium. The pressures brought to bear by the emigrants were ignored because they and their supporters made the mistake of declaring revenge. After the first reverses and the victories which followed, came new defeats, made more serious, in April 1793, by the treachery of Dumouriez; fearing for himself and dazzled by ambitious plans, he rebelled against the Convention. In the provinces the situation had already been serious for some time, both on account of the disastrous state of the economy and of the anarchy caused by the violent transfer of

Left: the end of the struggle between the Girondins and the Montagnards on May 31 1793. Among the Girondins is, in the centre, Hérault de Séchelles, hands outstretched. Behind, Fauchet has his right arm round Brissot. Against the pillar on the left, Vergniaud; in front of him "the handsome Pétion". Marat can be seen in front on the left.

power. For the last two years, the departments into
which France had just been divided had been the
scene of disorders. The shortage of provisions and the
increasingly high cost of living drove the starving
populace to attack shops, warehouses and markets.
Raiders organized themselves into bands. Even the
National Guard took advantage of the situation to
commit every conceivable abuse. The entire country
was torn by struggles between all classes and political
opinions. In Paris, on March 8, 9 and 10, the panic
aroused by military defeats led the sections of the
Commune to rebel against the Convention, which had
voted for a revolutionary tribunal; this was to have
been a new version of the one of August 1792 which
had been abolished by the Girondins; they hoped in
this way to bolster up the departments against the
Commune. The only result was that Paris grew
angrier still. In April 1793 a committee of Public
Safety was set up with nine members, none of them
Girondins. Now Robespierre's followers insisted that
it was imperative to inaugurate a temporary despotism of liberty, to finish once and for all the despotism of kings. This "temporary" was to become
permanent. The Girondins were blamed for the defeats
and for the treachery of Dumouriez, who had been
their general. They were the target of a new revolutionary "day" on June 2, as the King and earlier assemblies
had been in the past. Eighty thousand men surrounded
the Convention. Robespierre demanded the indictment of 22 Girondin deputies and Marat slowly read
out the names, until that moment the most eminent of
the Revolution. Anatole France was to entitle one of
his novels Les Dieux ont soif. The gods of the revolutionaries were not just thirsty; they were insatiable.

Left: Mme. Roland (of Heinsius) and Jean-Marie Roland de la Platière. Manon Phlipon was born in Paris in 1754. Cultured, intelligent and sensitive, she married Roland, a philosopher and philanthropist, in 1780 and encouraged him to go into politics. Minister of the Interior in March 1792, Roland had to resign on January 22, 1793, on the eve of the King's execution. When the Girondins fell he managed to escape to Normandy, where on learning of the death of his wife he killed himself. Mme. Roland was admired for her beauty, her energy and her logic. At her execution she is said to have cried: "Oh liberty, what crimes are committed in thy name!"

THE YOUNG GIRL WHO KILLED MARAT

Left: the assassination of Marat, from a contemporary print. Below: Robespierre entering Marat's room immediately after the murder. Bottom of the page: portrait of Marie-Anne-Charlotte de Corday d'Armot; a young admirer of the Girondins, she carried through her plan with the greatest determination. Lamartine called her the angel of the assassination. At the guillotine, on July 17, as the executioner was preparing to cover her eyes in the customary way, she protested: "Sir, I have the right to be curious. I have never seen it before now." After Marat's death a popular cult grew up round his memory. He was buried in the Panthéon, but his remains were later removed from there.

During the period when Paris was without bread Marat and Hébert denounced the hoarders and encouraged the populace to revolt. The Girondins accused Marat of incitement to murder and ordered his arrest on April 13, followed on May 24 by that of Hébert. The triumphal release of Marat, "the people's friend", and the subsequent acquittal of Hébert, both at the insistence of the Commune, were determining factors in the fall of the Girondins, although there were important remòte causes. Robespierre's sense of timing often made it seem that he was being dragged along by events. But now he chose to anticipate them and he was in the forefront with a clear incitement to rebel: "I call upon the people to rise up against corrupt deputies." There were plenty of these and the fact should be recognized. Danton, whose passions were women and money, now inveighed against "vile modernisation which is leading us back to despotism", but this time even his vehemence could not match the rage of the Paris sections. The outcome is well known. Robespierre was increasing his control and becoming more and more intolerant of opposition. Thereafter, his judgements and his suspicions were enough to sentence a man to death. After the "day" of June 2 feelings ran higher between Paris and the provinces, and the departments rebelled against the capital, in an attempt to throw off its dictatorship. The directors of 69 departments protested at the arbitrary actions of the "Mountain". In several cities the Convention's representatives were arrested. The uprisings in Lyons, Toulon and in the unsettled Vendée were the most disquieting because they were on both monarchic and religious grounds. A young Royalist, Charlotte Corday, assured herself of a place in history by taking positive action. Dissatisfied by the half-hearted reactions of the men of her native Caen, she determined to make her protest in a manner worthy of one of Plutarch's heroines. She calmly boarded a stage-coach and, on her arrival in Paris, made several attempts to reach the tribune of the Convention. Finally she got an audience with Marat at his home. He was in his bath, taking down the names of refugee deputies in Caen, at her dictation, when she drew a knife and stabbed him in the heart. Later she faced the guillotine with equal courage.

Below, top to bottom: the siege of Lyons (October 1793); the attack of the Vendéans on Nantes in June '93; the Loire drownings ordered by Carrier, a deputy of the Convention, at Nantes (Dec. 6–7, 1793). Opposite page: the battle of Hondschoote (Sept. 8, 1793) which enabled the French to raise the English siege of Dunkirk. The reprisals against the Lyons rebels were directed by Fouché and Collot d'Herbois. Not content with guillotining they ordered mass shootings. On October 12, 1793 the Convention decreed that the city should be razed to the ground and its name deleted from the records. The "noyades" of Nantes made Carrier notorious.

Marie Antionette went to the guillotine on October 16, 1793 (below, popular print). Sentence was pronounced by the Revolutionary Tribunal, whose effective power dated from September 5, 1793, when their numbers were increased to form four groups, two of which functioned simultaneously. The unfortunate ex-Queen was sentenced at 4 a.m. and executed at midday. The guillotine was now designated "Saint", the very word which had been deleted from the names of places and streets. Curiously, the Public Prosecutor, Fouquier-Tinville, was more closely linked to the Cordeliers and to the Committee of Public Safety than to the legalistic Robespierre.

NINETY–THREE: THE YEAR OF TRAGEDY

Below, top to bottom: mass shootings carried out at Lyons by order of Collot d'Herbois, a former actor and poet, (Dec. 14, 1793); the procurator of the Lyons Commune, Marie-Joseph Chalier, proposes the execution of 1,200 leading rebels (Feb. 6, 1793); republican troops recapture Toulon (Dec. 18, 1793). These prints depict incidents from the rebellions at Lyons and Toulon. The revolt in Lyons was provoked by the arrest and execution of the Montagnard Chalier. The situation got out of hand and troops were sent in by the Convention to deal with it. After the Toulon risings were crushed Fréron and Barras imposed savage penalties.

Quatre-vingt-treize, "93", is the title of Victor Hugo's famous novel dedicated to the Revolution. Why should the great poet and novelist choose this particular year to symbolize the fortunes of the Revolution? The fact is that 1793 really was the crucial year for the new-born republic; in modern times it might possibly be compared to the years of the "wartime Communism" of the Soviet revolution. It began with the treachery of Dumouriez, which put France in grave danger. There followed fresh defeats, further economic difficulties and more revolts in different parts of the country. The threat of more uprisings in the provinces was deliberately fostered by the Girondins but, far from saving them, this action precipitated their fall. After the insurrectionary "day" of June 2, the threat became reality; about two thirds of the departments were now in revolt against the oppressive dictatorship of Paris. But although the revolution was fighting for its life the Girondins proved quite unequal to the occasion. In this year of tragedy the great majority of Frenchmen were neither Girondins nor Montagnards but simply monarchists or revolutionaries. The strength of the "Mountain" lay in its ability to produce men of determination capable of saving both France and the Revolution. The decision, taken in April, to call up 300,000 men, between the ages of 18 and 40, into the army, led the peasants to continue their guerilla warfare, especially in the Vendée, and in August a "mass levy" became necessary. This finally gave the Revolution the only instrument which could save it: an army capable of opposing the coalition of foreign powers. Austria and Prussia, already at war against France, had now been joined, since February, by England and Holland and, more in sympathy than action, by Spain and Portugal, the rulers of Sardinia and Naples, the states of the German empire and Russia. By the end of this tragic year of '93 the French army was able to ensure for itself a crushing numerical superiority over the allies; a million men were mobilized, which in those days was an incredible achievement. It was this vast army which saved both republican France and the Revolution from the enemy without. The enemy within was supplied by the revolutionary government of the "Mountain".

HARSH REALITY
NECESSITATES
GOVERNMENT BY
COMMITTEE

Driven by sheer force of necessity, the Republic was forging the tools which would give it efficient government and at the same time keep the revolutionary fire blazing. So, in April, 1793, the first Committee of Public Safety was formed to be the Convention's instrument of government. While this work was going on, the Commune set up a Committee of Correspondence, designed to further its relations with other municipalities and to stimulate progressive action. The old constitution had become obsolete at the King's death and so it now became necessary to draft a new one; the new authorities were anxious that it should be perfect, for they were still obsessed with the idea of constitutional government. There were many debates on the subject, and during these discussions Robespierre had the chance to develop and explain his own political and ideological system more clearly. He envisaged the constitution as a manifesto of the declaration of the rights of the French people and he felt that it should be an ideal universal code acceptable and appropriate to all nations. His definition of the law of property as "the right of every citizen to enjoy and dispose of that portion of goods which the law guarantees him" is especially significant because it limits as well as affirms. However, the Constitution of Year I, as it was called, was destined to remain on paper, perhaps being far too perfect to be practical. In any case, there was to be a surfeit of proposed constitutions during the Revolution. All this provided material for endless discussion,

but other and graver problems troubled the Rebublic during the difficult scorching summer of '93. The Committee of Public Safety and its subsidiary committees were completely overhauled. This huge executive body, to which Robespierre was elected on July 27, 1793, shared its responsibilities with the Committee of General Security. The Committee of Public Safety administered the conduct of the war, diplomacy, supplies, control of the army and the application of all the new revolutionary laws. The Committee of General Security, which had its own secular branch in the revolutionary tribunals, was in charge of the police and the administration of justice. These two bodies were often in conflict and were, at times, directly opposed to one another, yet such was the force of Robespierre's character that he was able to establish and strengthen a virtual dictatorship over them both. Moreover he enjoyed the support of the insurrectionary Paris Commune and of the Jacobins, whose society was able to count on the help of hundreds of local organizations, all working in the provinces in harmony with the centre. In this government by committee Robespierre emerged increasingly as the high priest of the "Mountain", the self-styled "symbol of united patriotism and of the republican religion". His power grew, as it became apparent that only he could command respect from both the committee of Public Security and the committee of Public Safety and so unify them despite their rivalry.

Opposite page: inside a revolutionary committee in 1793 (from a drawing by the younger Fragonard). At the seat of the committee, which resembles an ordinary guard-room, can be seen (left) a citizen – perhaps an ex-aristocrat or bourgeois – with his wife and little girl, waiting hat in hand to present a document to the committee. There were normally 12 members in such committees, and at least 7 of these were required to be present in order to pass a resolution. This page, on the left: one of the best known portraits of Robespierre, by an anonymous artist. His shortsightedness gave him a somewhat cat-like look but this in no way detracted from his dignity. Above: meeting of the revolutionary tribunal during the trial of Brissot and other Girondin deputies.

47

TERROR BECOMES THE ORDER OF THE DAY

In September 1793 the Paris sections requested that "Terror should be the order of the day", and the Convention agreed. On October 10, at Saint-Just's suggestion, it decreed that "the provisional government of France shall be revolutionary until there is peace". To begin with, on September 17, there was published the law of suspects, loosely defined as "all those who by their actions, relationships, speeches and writings have become suspect in any way". All were liable to the death penalty. There was nevertheless a scruple of legality in all this work, above all where Robespierre was concerned; he was anxious to legitimize the actions of the *sansculottes*. This name was originally contemptuous but the *sansculottes* accepted it as a challenge and took pride in it. Robespierre stated a most important constitutional maxim: "It is the most sacred duty of a people whose rights are violated by its government to rebel". Sections and committees were authorized to arrest anyone. The departments were visited by "deputies on mission", acting for the Convention; invested with full powers, they arrested generals and "purged" administrators, and were backed up by the societies affiliated to the Jacobins. There were no half-measures. Now was the time to win or die. The revolutionary motto was "liberty or death" or "Liberty, equality or death". The grim words were heard on every side. The guillotine had become the "national leveller". This process was kept in motion by the revolutionary spirit, which thrust aside all obstacles, and also partly by the redistribution of wealth due to the confiscation of the property of those who were executed. There were those who had once been important people as well as humbler victims. Towards

Left: corridor of St. Lazare prison in 1793, by Hubert Robert (1733 – 1808). Like many artists Robert was an unwilling guest at this prison during the Revolution. More fortunate than most, he escaped on 9th Thermidor. Right: the so-called "furies" of the Revolution, rounded up by the Commune to act as a "chorus" at the executions.

Below: taking supplies to the Saint Lazare prisoners (detail from a painting by H. Robert). Most of the Parisian prisoners were confined in old convents that had been requisitioned for the purpose. In all their ordeals the aristocrats continued to observe their dignified etiquette of bygone days and to show a lordly indifference to their fate. Below right: a portrait of Antoine Lavoisier and (print on the left) his arrest while at work in his laboratory. Lavoisier, one of the founders of modern chemistry, was executed on May 8, 1794 (16 Floréal Year II) because he had once belonged to the farmers-general. Since 1790 he had been a member of the Weights and Measures commission. When a stay of execution was requested to enable Lavoisier to continue important research the president of the tribunal is reported to have said that "the Republic has no need of scientists". On the opposite page: David's portrait of Conventionist Milhaud shows the uniform worn by the "deputies on mission".

the end of August General Custine was executed; a
brave soldier who had formerly campaigned in
America, he had met defeat in the revolutionary war
against Europe. Then it was the turn of 22 Girondin
deputies, all eloquent speakers for their party.
Foremost among them was Brissot, towards whom
Robespierre was particularly ruthless. On an October
morning the condemned men sang *a Marseillaise* in
chorus in front of the scaffold and then Citizen
Sanson silenced their voices one by one. Madame
Roland, whose memoirs were barely completed,
faced death proudly and courageously, although in
private she had given way to tears. On November 8,
after requesting in vain to be allowed to set down for
the last time "the strange thoughts which pass through
my mind", she appeared dressed in white with her
long dark hair hanging down. She claimed the respect
due to a lady's last wish and was given leave to
advance her turn. In the same month of November the
astronomer, Bailly, was executed; he had been the
first president of the National Assembly and the
first mayor of Paris. For him the guillotine was
moved to a heap of dung on the river bank and there,
shivering with cold, he was beheaded in the rain. In
Paris, in the period from March 1, 1793 to July 27, 1794
alone there were 2,627 executions. This incredible
figure does not include the victims of the repressions
ordered by the commissioners to the provinces.

Left: the final roll-call of victims of the Terror. In the foreground André Chénier, who was born in Constantinople. in 1762. He mounted the scaffold on 7th Thermidor (July 25, 1794) after four months in prison. The fortunes of Chénier, France's greatest 18th century poet, reflect the times. He was arrested at Passy and condemned as a "suspect" because during a visit to his home he did not inform the landlords. His brother, Marie-Joseph, two years younger, wrote the words of one of the most beautiful hymns of the Revolution, "Le Chant du départ". This page, left: the suicide of Condorcet, philosopher and scientist, who was the leader of the committee of the constitution. He was arrested after the Jacobin victory and poisoned himself in prison on March 28, 1794. Below left: caricature of the laws of "maximum", introduced to control prices. Right: an anonymous print attacking Robespierre, who is seen guillotining the executioner after having guillotined all of France.

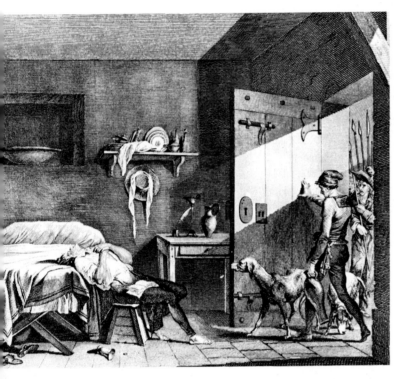

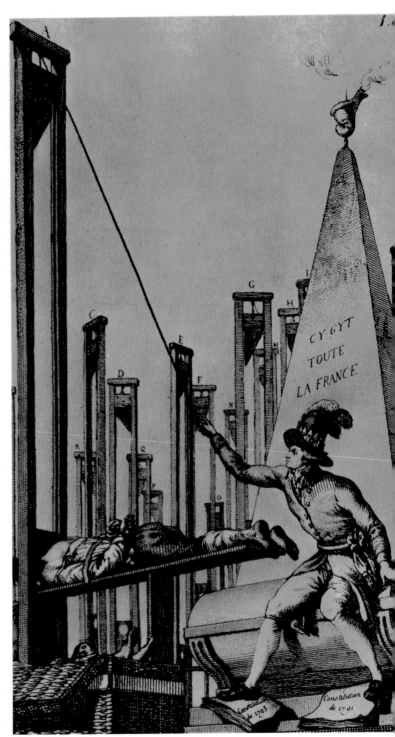

HE FINDS THE LOVE OF HIS LIFE

Left: Eléonore Duplay and (bottom of page) her father, the carpenter, Maurice Duplay. He left Gévaudan, a southern province in Languedoc, and settled in Paris in 1765; here he married a woman older than himself. His work brought him a certain prosperity. Below: the Duplay house in the rue Saint-Honoré, Paris.

With the passage of time Robespierre ceased to be the little lawyer from Arras, who alternated his professional duties with literary diversions at the Academy of the Rosati, but he remained basically a working man who rose early, drank milk for breakfast, took water with his wine at mealtimes and preferred to tire himself out with work rather than play. Since July 17, 1791, the day of the ferocious massacre at the Champ de Mars, he had lodged in rue Saint-Honoré, at the house of Maurice Duplay, a well-off carpenter. Here, close by the Jacobin Club and the Convention, Robespierre occupied a room above the workshop; it was papered in blue and looked out over the courtyard. This was his refuge. Although he was deeply engaged in public life he remained remarkably detached from everyday reality. Sheltered by the devout and watchful protection of his hosts, he worked from early until late, preparing his speeches and composing articles. The companionship of the Duplay family was tranquil and soothing. He was particularly fond of oranges, which he consumed greedily to counter his biliousness; they were the only luxury he permitted himself. Robespierre, so difficult to understand, adored by some and reviled by others, was possibly only able to be his real self within these walls, where he was sheltered by the love of this unpretentious family, all devoted to him. The household included four daughters and a son, as well as two adopted orphaned nephews. One of the girls was married to a lawyer from Issoire; another was to marry one of Robespierre's followers, who later committed suicide. One of the younger sisters, shy Eléonore, was engaged to Robespierre. Danton, with his customary rough wit, nicknamed her Cornélie Copeau: Cornelia for virtue and Copeau, meaning wood chip, because she was the daughter of a carpenter. She outlived her hero but her mother killed herself in despair. Eléonore Duplay was never able to take Robespierre's name but she remained faithful to his memory throughout her life. It is strange that Robespierre should have inspired such passion in women – being so reserved and remote, so dedicated to his mission in life, so ready in the face of danger, as he frequently repeated in his speeches and writings, to sacrifice himself that people might be saved.

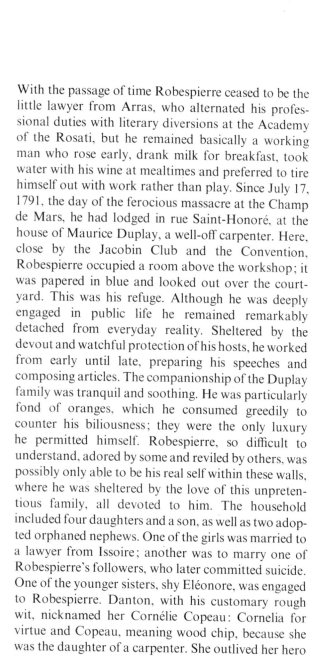

Right: Robespierre with a colleague at the Duplay house. He settled permanently with the Duplay family in the summer of 1791. He was fond of an ordered life and regularly took his dog for walks. He sometimes accompanied the daughters on their excursions. Elisabeth Duplay, the youngest sister, was married to a member of the Convention, Lebas, and committed suicide when Robespierre was arrested; she wrote: "He was our defender when Mamma scolded us". After supper he often read extracts from Corneille, Racine and Rousseau to the family.

Vendémaire

Nivôse

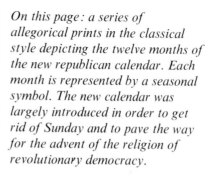

On this page: a series of allegorical prints in the classical style depicting the twelve months of the new republican calendar. Each month is represented by a seasonal symbol. The new calendar was largely introduced in order to get rid of Sunday and to pave the way for the advent of the religion of revolutionary democracy.

Messidor

Brumaire

Pluviôse

Germinal

Thermidor

Frimaire

Ventôse

Floréal

Fructidor

Prairial

THE BEAUTIFUL
NAMES OF THE
REPUBLICAN MONTHS

One of the first actions of the Convention had been to proclaim Year I of the Republic, to begin on September 22, 1792; the autumn equinox thus became New Year's Day. With the help of two mathematicians, Monge and Legrange, and suggestions from a poet, Fabre d'Églantine, a new calendar was inaugurated; it remained in force from October 5, 1793 until the 99th day of Year XIV December 31, 1805, thus outlasting the Republic. It was said to be more practical; in fact it was prompted by the desire to blot out the past. It seems complicated and without a comparative table it would be very difficult to equate the revolutionary dates with the "old style". The year had twelve months each of 30 days, plus 5 special "days of the *sansculottes*" dedicated to civic festivals. Every fourth year a sixth day was added to commemorate the Revolution. The months were divided into three

The allegorial print (above) was published under the title: "The people of France or the rule of Robespierre". Some verses underneath describe the fate of the French nation, doomed, it seems, to play blindman's buff without ever catching anything. The game is given grim significance by the presence of the symbolic figure of Death, on the right. The Terror was not confined to Paris; it spread throughout all the national territory until it became a movement increasingly controlled and directed from the top. The official departmental figures show

that 14,807 people were put to death by the tribunals or by the revolutionary commissions. To these must be added, apart from those who fell in the wars and rebellions, those who were summarily executed, an estimated 20,000. It is interesting to break down the total into percentages of the various classes who supplied the guillotine with heads. Some 6 per cent of these were aristocrats, 7 per cent were soldiers, 8 per cent were priests, 12 per cent were middle class and small landowners, 29 per cent labourers and servants and 38 per cent were farmworkers.

Aspects of republican life during the Jacobin dictatorship. Below (left): civil marriage and (right) divorce. Underneath: the inauguration of the fountain of the Regeneration. Right: the burning of the symbols of monarchy. These two ceremonies were held in Paris on August 10, 1793 as part of the festival of unity.

periods of ten days. The year began on the September equinox, 1 Vendémaire, which fell on either the 22, 23 or 24 of September. Saints' days were banned, since the calendar set out to eliminate the "prejudices of the throne and the altar". The French names for the months of the republican calendar are extremely melodious. They were selected by Fabre d'Églantine (he too ended on the guillotine). The names for the autumn months are soft and melancholy: Vendémaire, Brumaire, Frimaire; the winter months solemn and sonorous: Nivôse, Pluiôse, Ventôse; light sounds for spring: Germinal, Floréal, Prairial; rich and tuneful for summer: Messidor, Thermidor, Fructidor. To return to Robespierre; he was executed on 10th Thermidor, of the Year II (July 28, 1794). It was a tenth day and therefore a holiday and it was dedicated to the watering can.

Two very contrasting anti-Jacobin caricatures: the revolutionary patrol and the "cauldron of purification". These documents express two different moods. The first print carries the cynical inscription: "Friends, what Masses are offered to our courage. Let us leave the honours and get on with the looting".

ELIMINATION OF THE MADMEN

The caricature (below), published after the arrest of Hébert on March 14, 1794, carries the caption: "Père Duchesne is in a great rage". Le Père Duchesne was the title of a journal which by its violence and vulgarity did much to help the rise of Jacques-René Hébert in the spring of 1793. A member of the Cordeliers' club and standard bearer of the anti-religious struggle and the cult of Reason, Hébert with his followers advocated a violent social upheaval. Several corrupt deputies were attacked by them at the end of '93 and Robespierre turned against them. They attempted a coup d'état on March 4, 1794 but were arrested and executed on March 24, 1794.

The economic situation grew worse each day. The inflation got out of hand. The *assignats,* originally promissory notes exchangeable for national property, (chiefly that of the church) circulated like banknotes. The soldiers were short of most things, including shoes; Saint-Just and Lebas, on a mission to Strasbourg, ordered that shoes should be taken from the feet of 10,000 aristocrats and given to as many barefoot soldiers. Farmers hid their produce and speculators were often in league with men of influence. One can understand why a group of extremists to the left of the "Mountain" took upon themselves the label of "Madmen". Roux, together with Hébert and Chaumette, accused the Convention of starving the populace. To the law of suspects was now added that of the "maximum", the degree which fixed the maximum price of vital commodities without taking into account the value of the currency. It was followed by the even more unpopular "maximum" of wages. During this period Robespierre was feverishly busy. His motto seemed to be *"politique d'abord"*, politics above all. But he could not leave a clear field for the "Madmen"; rather he must push them further to the left. On February 26, 1794 (8 Ventôse Year II) he decided that property of persons recognized as enemies of the Republic should be confiscated. Immediately afterwards came the order that it should be distributed to needy patriots. The game was now over. Hébert's call to insurrection went unheeded. He was arrested with others of his group on the night of March 13-14 (22-23 Ventôse), brought before the tribunal as part of a batch of conspirators and foreign agents (always a good political ploy to smear an opponent) and executed on March 24 (4 Germinal). It was the end of the Cordeliers. All the same, an attempt had been made to relax the regime and calm the citizen shareholders. But the decrees of Ventôse and their imperfect enforcement indicated a tiny crack in the heart of the Committee of Public Safety. Robespierre underestimated the significance of this drama, which disorganized popular action and set loose a band of armed republicans empowered to hunt down suspects. It marked the beginning of a decline, for it gave the impression that the Terror was being used to keep a particular group of men in power.

Below: Danton and Desmoulins at the scaffold. To bring down Danton Robespierre briefed Saint-Just to make a report on the basis of which the joint committees of Public Safety and General Security decided, on March 30, 1794, to arrest Danton, Desmoulins and other members of the Convention. Danton, the standard-bearer of the Revolution in 1792, had instituted the revolutionary tribunal. Desmoulins had been largely responsible for the fall of the Girondins, by his attacks on Brissot and the "Brissotins" – though later he had shown more clemency. Opposite: Robespierre at the Convention. He remained faithful to the old style of dress.

Louis de Saint-Just (left, in the uniform of a Conventionist) was nine years younger than Robespierre and one of his most ardent followers. When 25 he was elected to the Convention, and became its president in February, 1794. From 1793 he belonged to the Committee of Public Safety, and he distinguished himself as military commissioner in Alsace. Right: Louise Gély, Danton's second wife, whom he married in June, 1793, and his son, Antoine, by his marriage to Gabrielle Charpentier.

A GREAT TRIBUNE'S FINAL INVECTIVE

Robespierre is often spoken of as a dictator, but, in fact, the only dictatorship established during the Terror was that of the Committee of Public Safety. The decree of December 4, 1793 (14 Frimaire Year II) laid down: "The National Convention is the supreme authority of government; all its appointed committees and public servants are under the direct supervision of the Committee of Public Safety". In reaffirming the authority of the Convention it was really emphasising the omnipotence of the Committee. At the centre of this the only men of any political account, apart from Robespierre, who was still its leading figure, were his two faithful lieutenants, Couthon and Saint-Just. The other members were limited to specific duties, as for example Carnot, later to earn the name of "organizer of victory". Once the "Madmen" of the Hébertist left were eliminated it became necessary to follow up with the suppression of the Dantonist *Indulgents* (as the Jacobins had rechristened them) of the right. Between the impetuous Danton and the impassive Robespierre, the ardent demagogue, corrupt but kindly, and the cold revolutionary, incorruptible to the point of inhumanity, there was personal antipathy and incompatibility. In December in *Le Vieux Cordelier,* his new journal, the *Indulgent* Camille Desmoulins had attacked the Reign of Terror and demanded the formation of a "Committee of Clemency". Six days after the execution of Hébert and his followers, the *Indulgents* were arrested in their turn and accused of conspiring against the Republic. Danton had also contributed to the gathering storm by exclaiming: "A hundred times better to be executed than to be the executioner". Perhaps he trusted to his popularity to protect him. When denounced before the revolutionary Tribunal he recovered all his old eloquence. It was necessary for Saint-Just, who had presented most of the case on a brief from Robespierre, to obtain a decree from the Convention on April 5, 1794 allowing judgement while preventing those who had "abused the national justice" from appearing in court. In this way Danton and his followers were effectively denied the opportunity to speak in their own defence. As he and the others were being taken to the scaffold on April 5, Danton struggled to his feet in the tumbril and shouted: "You'll soon follow me!"

The pictures on these pages show incidents from the war of 1794. *Below:* the Vengeur, *sunk by the English, enabled a convoy of grain from the United States to be brought in on June 8, 1794. Centre: the siege of Landrecies, Below: a young republican mother puts a group of Vendéans to flight by threatening* to blow up a powder barrel and sacrifice herself and her children. *Right: the battle of Fleurus by J.–B. Mauzaisse. After the victory of Wattignies (October 15–16, 1793) General Jourdan returned to Limoges to his drapery business. He was recalled by Carnot and Saint-Just, his victory at Fleurus gave Belgium to the French.*

NEW MEN BRING VICTORIES IN YEAR II

For Robespierre the struggles against enemies at home and abroad were two sides of the same coin. It was composed of War and Revolution and on both sides he saw the French nation rising against the forces of counter-revolution. Although formerly he had been opposed to the war declared by the Girondins, he now became the champion of war to the bitter end. On April 12, 1793, he demanded the "death penalty for anyone proposing to come to terms with the enemies of the Republic", and on June 18 he declared that "A nation which treats with its enemies on its own territory is a defeated nation and one which has renounced its independence." The mass levy had been proclaimed in August 1793 and now it was a question of finding new men to put at the head of the new army. "Three heroes will suffice to save the Republic. They are hidden somewhere in the ranks and we must have the will to find them", declared Robespierre on the rostrum of the Convention. While the commissioners to the fourteen revolutionary armies upheld and strengthened political control the professionals set to work to reconstruct the army, or rather create it. The greatest of these professionals was Carnot, an officer of genius who was brought into the Committee of Public Safety. Although at heart Robespierre was profoundly anti-military he did not hesitate to give credit to the new generals. Some of them, like Hoche, Augereau and Marceau, had risen from the ranks; others, like Desaix, Davout, Bonaparte and Pichegru, were young officers who had embraced the revolutionary cause; still others were volunteers who had made their mark, like Kléber, Moreau and Jourdan. By spring 1794 France had turned her back on the year of tragedy and the defeats of '93. Now the revolutionary armies – already known abroad as the forces of Robespierre – won victory after victory. Counter-revolutionary Europe could only look on in amazement at this miraculous and inexplicable change. Executing Carnot's strategy to perfection, Pichegru and his 160,000 men moved in to support the 230,000 who, under Jourdan, formed the army of the Sambre and Meuse. At Fleurus on June 26, 1794 the enemy was defeated. On July 23 the soldiers of the Revolution fought their way into Antwerp.

Some aspects of the Festival of the Supreme Being, initiated by Robespierre. Above: the ceremony in progress at the Champ de Mars, from a painting by Machy. Right: the procession of the Paris sections. Far right: view of the national gardens with scenery painted by David, from a print of a drawing by Monnet. On the morning of 20 Prairial Year II (June 8, 1794), Paris was decked with flowers. Robespierre made the mistake of ordering the Convention to attend and they received him in a silence which the cheers of the crowd only served to emphasize. The procession's route was from the Tuileries to the Champ de Mars.

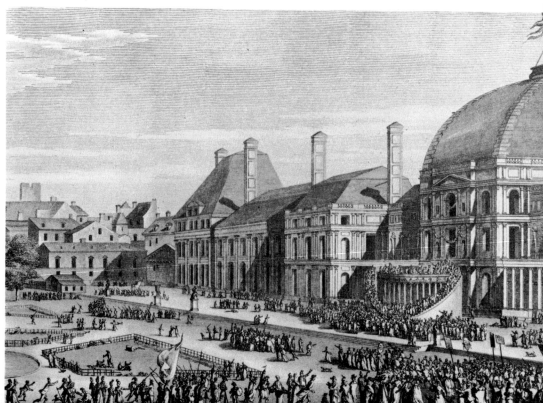

ATHEISM GOES UP IN FLAMES AT THE FESTIVAL OF THE SUPREME BEING

Robespierre dreamed of a perfect society. He sought to attain it with the inexorable rigour of an intellectual who has been flung headlong into politics. It was to be a just society, but to be perfect it must also be animated by a religious spirit and find its fulfilment in worship. But which religion? Certainly not that of the refractory priests opposed to the Republic. Nor that of the priests introduced into the new régime; there was certainly no need to encourage them, for, having thrown their cassocks to the winds, they were now distinguished for their anti-Christian fervour. He envisaged a belief in the homeland and a Supreme Being which would take precedence over other creeds without necessarily eliminating them. Among the reasons for Robespierre's aversion to the Hébert extremists had been some which were specifically social and political. During the economic setbacks of wartime he had sought to protect the artisans and small shopkeepers and declared that the extremists, "by destroying trade, wanted to starve the people". He had also felt an inner repugnance for their avowed atheism. He had warned of the dangers of violent "de-Christianization" which was already changing into brutal persecution. Some deputies on mission had ordered crosses to be torn down. One such was Fouché, though possibly this was because he was an unfrocked priest. At the entrances to cemeteries they had written: "Death is an eternal sleep". On November 10, 1793 (20 Brumaire) the Commune ordered the celebration of an idolatrous festival of Liberty and Reason. Liberty was personified by a well-built dancer from the Opéra. Several days later the Commune ordered the closure of "all churches and temples in Paris, of whatever religion or creed". A stop had to be put to all this. By December 6, 1793 (16 Frimaire, Year II) Robespierre got the Convention to pass a law forbidding "any violence or measure against religious freedom". In an impassioned speech he merged love of the homeland with religion and recalled those who had given their lives for the Revolution, and declared: "If the existence of God and the immortality of the soul were mere dreams they would still be the finest creations of the human spirit". The sequel to this speech was the law unanimously approved by the Convention on 18 Floréal, of

Opposite page: a revolutionary allegory in honour of Jean-Jacques Rousseau, by Jeaunat de Bertry. Below the likeness of the writer is the eye, symbol of the Supreme Being. The obelisk on the left is dedicated to Galileo. An inscription on the stones on the right extols the reform of customs. In the background, scarcely visible, is the guillotine. Below: allegory in honour of the cult of the Supreme Being. The inscription reads: "When atheism fades the wisdom of the French people appears". Bottom: Cécile Renault is arrested near Robespierre's house (June 22, 1794). Sixty other people were beheaded with her, all in the red shirts of murderers.

which article 1 says: "The French people recognize the Supreme Being and the immortality of the soul". The festival of the Supreme Being, designed by the painter, David, was celebrated on June 8, 1794. The Parisians rose early, some out of curiosity, others from public duty. After yet another rehearsal of the hymn which began "Father of the Universe, supreme wisdom," the sections moved in procession to the Tuileries, where a green amphitheatre had been embellished with statues, flowers and banners. A salvo of guns at 10 o'clock announced the arrival of the deputies in their dark blue suits with tricolour sashes and plumed hats, each holding a bunch of flowers. They were preceded by Robespierre, the elected president of the Convention, who wore a lighter suit and carried two bunches of flowers, one in each hand. After his oration he advanced on the straw effigy of atheism and set fire to it. From its ashes rose the image of wisdom, which was meant to be incombustible. Unfortunately, the burning of atheism, which served as its cover, had slightly singed it. The procession re-formed and headed for the Champ de Mars where a symbolic mountain had been erected, and the Members of the Convention duly ascended it. Hymns sung at the Tuileries were repeated and the festival ended with more singing. It marked the climax of Robespierre's career. But seeing the seven or eight deputies escorting him as he moved to set fire to the effigy of atheism, some onlookers were heard to comment: "Look at his lictors".

COMPLETE ISOLATION

Below left: the troops of the Convention attack the town hall, seat of the Paris Commune, to carry out the decree outlawing Robespierre and his followers. At the end of the sitting of 9 Thermidor, which lasted five hours, the Convention arrested Robespierre, his brother, Couthon, (who was then a paralytic), Lebas and Saint-Just. The Commune rebelled and freed the prisoners, who were taken to the town hall. Half an hour after midnight they were all outlawed. Below: On the rostrum Tallien, brandishing a dagger, prevents Robespierre from speaking at the sitting of 9 Thermidor (from a popular print of the period).

How could the man who in 1791 had opposed capital punishment support the notorious Prairial law of June 10, 1794? Cross-examination was disallowed, defence and counsel excluded. It was sufficient for the tribunal to believe they had a criminal before them for him to be condemned. The stark fact is that between April and July 2,100 heads fell in Paris, 1,376 of them between June 10 and July 27. While it was possible to grumble about the "Factions" dissatisfaction had centred on them. Now Robespierre was in the open. By his moral aloofness he had isolated himself. Everything seemed to conspire against him. He was ridiculed because the "Mother of God", Cathérine Theot, had proclaimed him the new Messiah; there were attempts on his life, as when Cécile Renault sought an audience with him while concealing "two small knives". There was certainly a conspiracy against him – and it was chiefly a conspiracy of fear. But as one of his biographers maintains: "No people, no nation ever deposed its leaders without at least the tacit consent of the majority". The dissent within the Committee of Public Safety, the hostility of the Committee of General Security and his own loss of will-power all worked against him. For almost a month he shut himself up at the Duplay's house, where documents were brought for his signature. Even the great festival of the Supreme Being, falling as it did on the feast of Corpus Christi, had both scandalized the pious and made hardened atheists laugh. He had also made the psychological error of failing to realize that the people had had enough. With the revolution triumphant they felt the time had

Portrait de Robespierre fait à la plume, par perseval Grand maison, à la séance du 9 thermidor.
(Les mots sont de la main de M. de Crugerville à qui Perseval Grandmaison donna ce dessin)

Left: profile of Robespierre drawn by Conventional Perseval-Grandmaison during the session of 9 Thermidor. Below: the arrest of Robespierre, from a contemporary English print. This seems at first sight to support the theory of attempted suicide but today it is accepted that the shot was fired by another hand, perhaps that of a gendarme. The sections still loyal to the Commune had dispersed after fruitless hours of waiting during a night of torrential rain, leaving Robespierre and his followers still arguing, and Conventional Barras, a future member of the Directory, had no difficulty in entering the town hall, followed by several gendarmes and other armed men.

come to pause. But would this moment ever come while there was Robespierre? The epilogue was swift. On July 26 (8 Thermidor, Year II) Robespierre mounted the rostrum of the Convention, threatening to punish traitors and to purge the Committees and even the Convention itself. Next day, 9 Thermidor (July 27), the meeting began at eleven a.m. Hall and platforms were packed. Robespierre tried to speak at least eleven times; neither he nor his followers were permitted to do so. The suspension of parliamentary privilege, enforced by the Prairial law, now worked against him, as did the laws of indictment which he had hoped to obtain against his enemies. Instead, the vote was unanimously against him, Couthon, Saint-Just, the younger Robespierre and Lebas. At half past three they left under escort. But there was a last hope – the Commune. Robespierre and his followers reached the town hall. Confused commands created disorder. Robespierre was not good at making decisions and there was no time for reflection. By about seven p.m. they had assembled some 3,500 men, but during the night they grew tired of waiting and dispersed. At two a.m. on the 10 Thermidor (July 28) the men of the Convention arrived. A gendarme called Méda boasted that he had shot Robespierre. Lebas committed suicide. The younger Robespierre struggled through a window and others also escaped but were recaptured. At five p.m. the tumbrils left the Conciergerie carrying the first batch of 22 condemned men. Altogether 108 people paid with their lives for their devotion to Robespierre. Others, like Madame Duplay, committed suicide. The Terror was ending in slaughter.

Below: Robespierre lying wounded in the lobby of the Committee of Public Safety (contemporary print). In the early hours of 10 Thermidor soldiers and armed citizens carried him on a board to the seat of the Committee. Here he was laid on a table with blood trickling from his wound onto his shirt.

Right: portrait of Robespierre's brother, attributed to Boilly. Beyond it: Robespierre's severed head (woodcut). The title of the print accuses him of being "the modern Catiline". An inscription below reads: "I have betrayed the French people and the Divinity. I am dying on the scaffold. I deserve my fate".

Far right: execution of Robespierre (English print). After identification the 22 prisoners, including Robespierre, were taken from the Conciergerie in three tumbrils in the late afternoon of July 28. They took an hour and a half to reach the guillotine. The crowds cheered. Other groups followed on successive days.

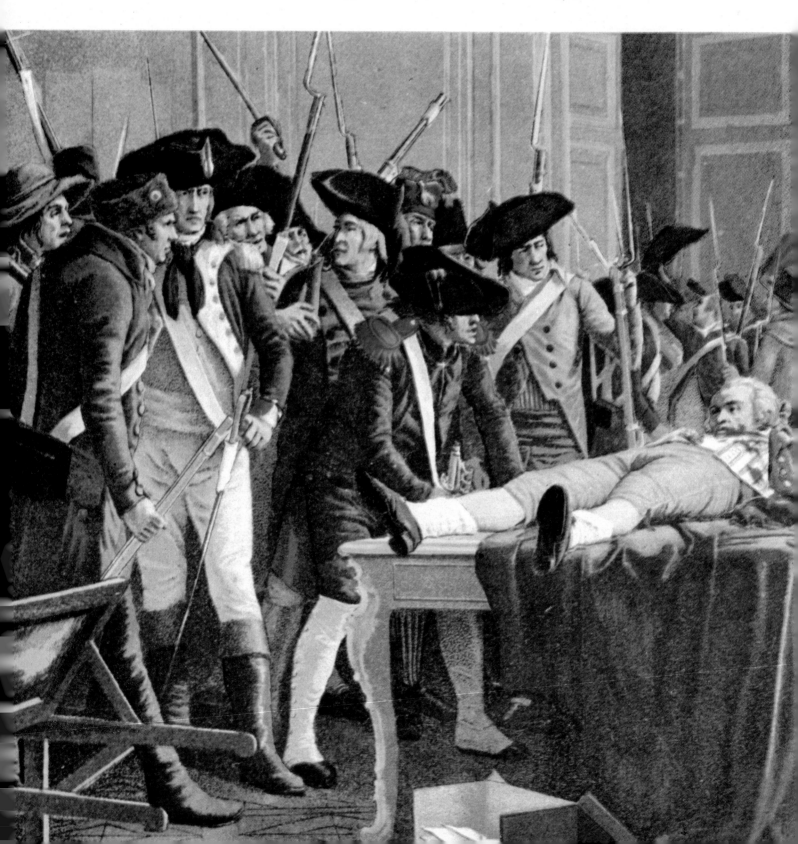

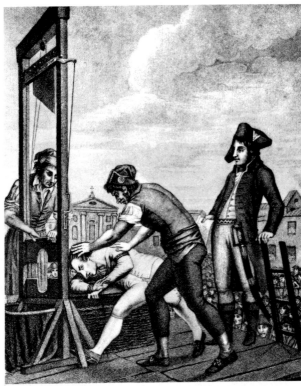

When it was decided to banish Aristides from ancient Athens, one of the voters said: "I am voting against Aristides because I am tired of hearing him called 'the Righteous'". So also the French had wearied of hearing Robespierre called "The Incorruptible". Four lines of verse will serve as an epitaph: *"Maximilien de Robespierre – incorruptible sans repit – il fallut le mettre sous terre – pour qu'enfin il se corrompit"*; Maximilien de Robespierre, incorruptible uninterrupted, must be buried underground, so that at last he may be corrupted". But with him the Revolution too was buried for he had been its personification during his life. Robespierre predicted the doom of France and of the Revolution: "Victory does nothing but arm ambition, reawaken pride and hollow out with its own bright hands the tomb of the Republic . . . Loosen the reins of Revolution for a moment and you will see military dictatorship taking over and the leader of the factions overthrowing the reviled representatives." Of his own family, his younger brother was overthrown with him. His sister, Charlotte, outlived him until 1834. She took his part even though there had not always been harmony between them; the Duplay family had guarded their distinguished guest with jealous care and she was not always able to reach him. However, the personal relationships of Robespierre and those near to him have a limited importance. He is remembered as a figurehead and as an example of virtue, virtue as he spoke of it and as it is understood in the old Roman use of the word; strength of mind in the service of a mission, which demands and accepts total sacrifice.

A DRAMATIC DOCUMENT

Of all the documents on the life of Robespierre the one reproduced here is the most dramatic. It is the appeal for help which the Executive Committee, the centre of the rebellious Paris Commune, drew up on the night of 9 Thermidor. Here is the text in translation: "Courage, patriots of the Section des Piques. Liberty is triumphant. Already those whose tenacity struck fear into the traitors are at liberty. Everywhere the people are proving themselves worthy of their own vigour. The meeting place is the Commune. Here the gallant Hanriot will carry out the orders of the Executive Committee, created to save our native land".

The "brave" Hanriot, whose name is quoted in the document, was the commander of the Paris National Guard. Already, however, the Convention had deprived him of his powers for refusing to carry out orders. Precious hours had been wasted. It was as if the accusations of despotism publicly hurled at Robespierre had paralysed him. He had been a dictator in fact but decisions were always taken jointly; appearances had always been preserved. Now this armour of legality with which Robespierre had surrounded his actions could no longer protect him. His whole world was smashed. This can surely be the only reason why he reluctantly decided to append his signature to this paper. He did not get beyond the first two letters before his own blood stained what might well be called his death certificate.

For Robespierre there was no middle way: he had to be either exalted or reviled. This is still his fate today. There is everything to be said against him. He can be reproached for arrogance and coldness, for indecision and for desiring good while allowing evil to take its course. There is everything to be invoked in his defence, above all his desperate longing to conquer for France and the Revolution, and his immense faith in humanity. "I shall await the tardy assistance of time, which must avenge betrayed humanity and peoples who are oppressed." These are his words. Also his are the few verses, recorded by his sister, in which he expresses his fear of "dying for the people and being abhorred by them". After the clamour against Robespierre had died down the "persecuted patriot" was glorified wherever there was a popular movement. In time his enemies were to recognize his good faith. Too often respect for the man himself is accompanied by disregard for the work he accomplished. But this is what counts and what will endure. How could Robespierre's name be erased from the French Revolution which, in its most tragic phase, found in him its personification? How could he be excluded from the magnificent events which were destined to inspire so much of history? Let us never forget: when he died the conscience of the Revolution perished with him.

1758 – May 6: born at Arras, son of François and Jacqueline Carraut.
1764 – death of his mother.
1768 – death of his father.
1769 – wins a scholarship to study at school of Louis-le-Grand in Paris.
1780 July 31: finishes his studies in law.
1781 graduates in law. Returns to Arras to go into legal practice.
1783 – November 15: received into the Academy of Arras.
1785 – November 15: becomes a member of the literary society of the Rosati in Arras.
1788 – presents himself as candidate to the States-General.
1789 – April: rioting in Paris in the St. Antoine quarter. May: Jacobin club founded. May 5: convocation of the States-General at Versailles. Robespierre, elected representative, takes part. June 17: deputies of the Third Estate form themselves into National Assembly. June 20: Tennis Court Oath. June 23: Assembly meets again in solemn session in the presence of the King. July 9: National Assembly takes the name of Constitutional Assembly and begins to draw up the constitution. July 12: first popular risings at Palais Royal. July 13: formation of bourgeois militia. July 14: capture of the Bastille. August 4: deputies from the nobility propose the abolition of feudal rights to the Assembly. August 26: Assembly pass the Declaration of the Rights of Man. October 5: women of Paris march on Versailles. October 6: the King is compelled to leave Versailles for Paris. October 16: the Assembly also transfers to Paris. October 21: martial law imposed by the bly to end the disorders. Robespierre votes against it.

1790 – March 31: Robespierre is nominated president of the Jacobin Club. July 14: festival of the Federation at the Champ de Mars.

1791 – April 2: death of Mirabeau. May: Robespierre is appointed public prosecutor to the Paris tribunal. June 21: attempted flight of the King. June 22: arrest of the King at Varennes. June 25: return to Paris amid hostile crowds. July 17: in accordance with martial law soldiers fire on the crowd during disorders at the Champ de Mars. September 30: final sitting of the Constituent Assembly. October 1: first meeting of the Legislative Assembly. November 29: repressive measures against non-juror priests.

1792 – from March to June political power is in the hands of the Girondins. April 15: celebration of the Festival of Liberty. April 20: declaration of war on the "King of Hungary and Bohemia". June 10: Paris representatives go to the Tuileries. August 3: petition for the deposition of the King by the Paris sections. August 10: setting up of the Insurrectionary Commune of Paris. Attack on the Tuileries. The King and his family are taken to the Assembly, which announces that he has been deposed and calls for the election of a convention by universal suffrage. September: Danton dominates the "provisional executive Committee". September 2: Prussian troops capture Verdun. September 2-6: the September Massacre. September 12: Louis XVI the prisoner of the Commune. September 20: revolutionary troops defeat the Prussians at Valmy. Final session of the Legislative Assembly. September 21: first meeting of the National Convention. Robespierre is elected to the

Convention as one of the Paris representatives. September 22: "Year One of the Republic" starts. November 6: revolutionary troops beat the Austrians at Jemappes. December 11: the trial of the King begins.

1793 – January 15-20: Louis XVI is condemned to death. January 21: the King is guillotined. March 3: popular rising in Vendée. April 5: formation of the first "Committee of Public Safety". May 31 – June 2: the Girondins are expelled from the government. July 13: assassination of Marat. July 27: Robespierre, triumphing over his adversaries, becomes a member of the Committee of Public Safety. August: general conscription. September 5: beginning of the Terror. September 17: the Convention passes the law of Suspects. September 29: the "maximum" law is approved. October 9: capitulation of Lyons which had rebelled against the dictatorship. October 16: execution of Marie Antoinette. October 31: execution of leading Girondins.

1794 – March 13–14: arrest of the Hébertists. March 24: execution of Hébert. March 29–30: arrest of the Dantonists. April 5: execution of Danton. May 8: apotheosis of Robespierre during the festival of the Supreme Being. June 10: suppression of all legal rights of accused persons. Beginning of the Terror. June 26: the revolutionary armies defeat the coalition armies at Fleurus. July 26-27: Robespierre's enemies join together and provoke his fall. Robespierre is imprisoned but freed by the rebellious mob. Remaining in Paris on the night of July 27-28, he is arrested and wounded at the town hall. July 28: he goes to the guillotine.

PORTRAITS OF GREATNESS

General Editor
ENZO ORLANDI

Text by
LUIGI MARIO PIZZINELLI

Translator
BARBARA THOMAS

Published 1968 by
The Hamlyn Publishing Group Ltd
London · New York · Sydney · Toronto
Hamlyn House, The Centre,
Feltham, Middlesex
© 1965 Arnoldo Mondadori Editore
Translation © 1968 by
The Hamlyn Publishing Group Ltd.
Printed in Italy by
Arnoldo Mondadori, Verona